OLD BUDE

by
Joan Rendell

This book is dedicated to the memory of the ketch Ceres, *a dear 'old friend' when I was a child, making every ?*

Summerleaze Beach

Bude

St. Margaret's Hotel - Bude

Summerleaze Beach

The Bathing Pool

© Joan Rendell 2001
First published in the United Kingdom, 2001,
by Stenlake Publishing
Telephone / Fax: 01290 551122

ISBN 1 84033 173 9

THE PUBLISHERS REGRET THAT THEY CANNOT SUPPLY
COPIES OF ANY PICTURES FEATURED IN THIS BOOK.

ACKNOWLEDGEMENTS

I am deeply indebted to Mr Harvey Kendall, curator of Bude Museum, and Mrs Gill Kendall, archivist at Bude Museum, for so willingly making available to me a selection of historic photographs from the museum collection and for providing background information to these. My thanks also to the Launceston and Bude branches of the Cornwall County Library for use of the facilities in the reference section of the libraries, and to Mr Peter Truscott and Mr Ray Shaddick for valuable information.

Extensive flooding at Nanny Moore's Bridge in 1903. The bridge takes its name from a widow called Moore who lived in the old millhouse in the nineteenth century. She was known as a 'dipper', a contemptuous name for those who practised the Baptist faith. However, in the summertime Nanny Moore occupied herself with duties as a bathing attendant and her 'dipper' title may have originated from that, as her job involved assisting people into the water. In winter she nursed the sick. She died in 1853 and is buried in St Michael's churchyard in Bude. It is said that in 1822 there were only seven houses in Bude, most of them being near Nanny Moore's Bridge.

INTRODUCTION

Bude is built on very ancient foundations, having been settled since at least the Bronze Age (there are Bronze Age barrows on Maer Down and other sites). In the sixteenth and seventeenth centuries it was no more than a fishing village consisting of a few fishermen's cottages, a manor house and a tide mill – a small community cut off from the world in its isolation and inaccessibility.

During this period the powerful Arundel and Grenville families held sway in the area and as was the wont in those days their power and authority were total and unyielding. Everything revolved around them, their lands and their properties. It was a feudal existence, but the people of Bude knew no other. The River Neet marked the boundary between Grenville and Arundel lands and both sides guarded their property fiercely.

In the eighteenth century Bude largely relied on fishing and was also a port of some importance. *The Universal British Directory* of 1791 records considerable trade in the exporting of corn, particularly oats, to different parts of the UK and vast quantities of bark to Ireland for use in tanning. Coal and salt were imported from Wales and Bristol respectively, as well as miscellaneous cargoes. Smuggling and wrecking were rife at the time. The coastline around Bude is littered with wrecks; the cruel rocks and deceptive tides having claimed many, many victims over the years.

A travel writer of 1859 described Bude as 'a small but growing watering place'. By this time the power of the Arundels had declined and things were beginning to change. Their lands had come into the possession of the Acland family, who proved to be a tremendous stimulus to Bude. Sir Thomas Acland was the driving force largely responsible for the development of the town. He was one of those instrumental in promoting and using the Bude Canal and he had his own wharf alongside it. He was also the instigator of several valuable amenities for the town. In the first half of the nineteenth century Lord Clinton and Lord Carteret also acquired land in the vicinity of Bude and the area became unrecognisable from that which Richard Carew had surveyed and documented in the seventeenth century. There is still a Carteret Road in the town. (Carew was an Elizabethan writer and chronicler whose best-known work was his *Survey of Cornwall*, published in 1602.)

The Bude Canal, on which work started in 1819, was a marvel of engineering of its time and did much to boost the importance of Bude as a port and town. Sadly, the arrival of the London & South Western Railway's line in 1898 killed it as a commercial undertaking and today what remains of it from Bude to Hele Bridge, Marhamchurch is used only for recreational purposes. The Bude Canal Society, formed in recent years, has done much to restore the section of the barge canal to Hele Bridge and the feeder arm from the reservoir at Tamar Lake, but most of the narrow tub boat canal in the hinterland has been lost forever to farming land and housing.

The town is still officially called Bude Haven, and its large schools continue to use that name, even though today most people and organisations – including the Post Office – have dropped the 'Haven.'

In 1899 the then popular *Cornish Magazine*, edited by A. T. – later Sir Arthur – Quiller-Couch, published an article entitled 'How to Develop Cornwall as a Holiday Resort'. Nothing changes, because the same issues are being discussed today, but what a furore that article caused in 1899! Some of the responses to it were very favourable, others were downright hostile – and insulting! A Miss J. H. Findlater wrote to the magazine that 'by promiscuous and unrestrained building Bude has been turned into a perfect eyesore'. She continued: 'Great rows of cheaply run up lodging houses stand in tiers on the cliffside and every abomination of the jerry builder is to be seen here to the greatest advantage'. Warming to her subject, Miss Findlater went on to say: 'Doubtless Bude will have its day and cease to be fashionable and another Bude, worse than the first, will rise on the now untouched wildness of the splendid western shores'.

A more acerbic assessment of any place could hardly be imagined, but fortunately Miss Findlater's views were not shared by everybody. *An Illustrated Itinerary of the County of Cornwall*, published half a century earlier in 1853, much more politely described Bude as 'a bathing place where retirement and quiet may be found in a degree seldom experienced by the anomalous towns generally so styled'. Perhaps at that time Miss Findlater's so-called 'jerry building' had not yet commenced.

For a very long time Bude has been famous for its fine sea bathing and splendid beaches, and it is these which attract so many holidaymakers today. Bude is now a modern seaside town offering a host of amenities and facilities.

Neighbouring Stratton is very different from Bude and retains much of its old-world charm and atmosphere, with its narrow streets and old houses clustered around the fine parish church of St Andrew, where the father of the famous vicar of Morwenstow, the Reverend Robert Stephen Hawker, was once vicar, and where R. S. lived as a boy.

Chroniclers of the past have pictured Stratton as a rather inhospitable place, but by the beginning of the twentieth century travel writers were being far more magnanimous and Stratton came in for some modest praise.

The manor of Stratton was recorded in the Domesday Book and the discovery of a dated stone during a church restoration in the 1870s proved that a church existed there in Norman times. (Nearly all Cornish churches of any note were 'restored' in the nineteenth century, resulting in many cases in them being spoilt, although St Andrew's did not fare too badly.) The font of St Andrew's is Norman, as is a fragment of a holy water stoup in the south porch. At one time the town had a thriving pannier market, and was a centre of commerce for people from many miles around, but all that disappeared at the turn of the twentieth century.

Perhaps Stratton's greatest claim to fame is the Battle of Stamford Hill, which took place during the Civil War in the seventeenth century. The site of the battle is marked by a rather curious monument comprising an arch surmounted by what is reputed to be a pinnacle from Poughill Church. There is also a commemorative plaque which records the famous battle of 16 May 1643, when Sir Bevil Grenville's Cornish army defeated the Earl of Stamford's forces.

The Tree Inn, a former Elizabethan manor house where the Stratton giant Anthony Payne is said to have lived and died, is now a very popular hostelry and retains many interesting old features. Stratton is linked to Bude by modern ribbon development but the old town is little changed and a complete contrast from the hustle and bustle of Bude in the holiday season. The two towns are linked in many ways but are totally different from each other, a rather endearing trait.

Peter Trick was a Stratton character of many years ago. He lived in the workhouse there for longer than anyone could remember and he had a curious obsession – he loved rats and was said to be able to communicate with them. This picture was taken in the early 1900s.

Flooding along the Crescent in the 1950s. This area is very prone to flooding and in the 1960s the river was straightened in an effort to improve the situation, although bad floods occurred soon after the work was carried out and local people claimed that the straightening had been a factor, saying that the Neet should have been left a winding river. Particularly bad flooding occurred on several occasions in the late 1990s. The 'lake' on the left is the site of the town's main car park.

The Triangle after the Great Blizzard of 20 March 1891. According to the *Post & Weekly News*, 'Suddenly on the Monday night the wind veered round to north east and the whole area of England was visited by a great snowstorm. The seas which surrounded the British Coast were swept by terrific gales. Southern counties, notably Devon and Cornwall, have for the most part been cut off from the outside world.' Today the Triangle looks nothing at all like it did in the nineteenth century. Road widening has swept away all the old cottages and there are now flower beds in the centre, while the site of the former Bude Hotel is now occupied by Lloyds Bank. This site was leased by the Thynne family in 1780 for the building of what was at first known as the Bewd Inn.

During the Big Freeze of February 1963 the River Neet froze over, and here ice is shown piling up by Nanny Moore's Bridge. The spectacle attracted quite a few local sightseers who had never seen the river frozen to such an extent before. Although a nineteenth century writer described Bude as not suffering from an east wind and having a balmy climate, it is obviously not always so. A newspaper report of 31 December 1874 records that 'at Bude on Wednesday the snowstorm was most severe'.

The Strand in the late 1870s. Until the wall was built along this attractive stretch of road the land sloped gently to the River Neet. Dwelling houses, an inn and a warehouse stood where there are now shops, a shopping arcade and hotels. This picture shows the original Globe Hotel; its successor, which was built in 1903, is still in existence and can be seen (with flag flying) on page 10.

An early view of the Strand. The Petherick family has been prominent in Bude since the nineteenth century. John Petherick was the first member of the family to settle in the town in 1841. He was a farmer, and Richard Petherick was a farm labourer. Henry Petherick became well-known as a china seller and merchant in the town in 1861 and by 1881 Pethericks were familiar as coal and general merchants over a wide area. They were also a seafaring family and owned the ketch *Ceres* through four generations. Richard Walter Petherick was a master mariner and in 1891 Henry Petherick was recorded as a member of the crew of the famous ketch. William and Walter Petherick were both merchants and seamen, and the family continued as merchants well into the twentieth century. The firm had warehouses and its own wharf by the Bude Canal.

Strand (looking down), Bude

Since this picture of the Strand was taken in the 1920s a number of shopfronts have been replaced and modernised and some buildings demolished. Most notable among the new buildings is the Strand Hotel with its very modern facade. The slate hung Carriers Inn is still a popular hostelry on the Strand, patronised by both locals and visitors. It was taken over by a carrier, one Thomas Heal, in the 1840s, hence its name which has never changed. Although the road was still pretty rough in the 1920s, lighting had been improved. Bude 'came into light' during the nine months up to midsummer 1878 when £25.19.9 was spent on lighting the main thoroughfares with oil. This included the purchase of five new lamps and posts.

The Strand and River Neet in the 1930s. In October 1862 the sailing ship *Bencoolen* was wrecked off Bude within a few yards of the shore. The loss of 24 men in the disaster ranks it as one of the worst shipping disasters off the north Cornish coast. The ship left Liverpool bound for Bombay on 13 October 1862 with a crew of 32, plus a ship's boy. In an unexpected gale it lost its foremast and sprang a serious leak. Captain Chambers, the master, was so devastated that he started drinking in an attempt to steady his nerves and made for what he thought was Milford Haven. In fact the ship was approaching Bude, where it grounded broadside. Chambers was said to be drunk by this point. The local rescue team went out with the rocket apparatus but the latter was put out of action by a gigantic wave. The ship's carpenter bravely tried to swim ashore with a line but was almost immediately drowned. A group of volunteers tried to put out in a lifeboat but were quickly driven back. The crew manhandled the ship's raft into the sea and 27 men scrambled aboard. *The West Briton* newspaper reported that the raft was washed onto the rocks and of the twelve men found on it only six were alive. Those on the raft were rescued with great difficulty, despite being only a cable's length from Bude breakwater. The *Bencoolen* had been carrying a cargo of telegraph poles, wires and cables, and what was salvaged from the vessel was put to use locally. Telegraph poles were used for the building of a barn (inset), while thick wire was threaded through posts to form the fence along the Strand, visible in this picture.

Mrs Foster Mellior laid the foundation stone of the Grenville Hotel on 15 November 1909 and on 18 June 1910 the *Post & Weekly News* reported that 'Bude's new hotel is to open on 7th July'. It was described as having been built to the most modern plans, prepared by one of London's leading architects, and the furnishings and appointments were said to be as comfortable as artistic. The Grenville was under the management of Mr H. Link, who had formerly been assistant manager at the Cecil Hotel in London and had worked at the Carlton Hotel (also in London) for four years. Bude's new hotel was said to command the finest sea views in the district and had beautiful grounds. Well-known guests included band leader Henry Hall and a number of other show business personalities. The Grenville closed as a hotel in the 1990s and is now run as an outdoor adventure centre for young people.

BUDE FROM HARTLAND TERRACE

The turreted tower with the flag flying from it is The Castle, former home of Sir Goldsworthy Gurney, inventor of, among other things, the Bude Light. It is now the town council offices. Bude Canal can be seen in front of the attractive canalside properties of Hartland Terrace, with St Michael's Church to the left of the picture. Prior to the construction of the canal huge sand dunes stretched right across to The Castle.

The top of Belle Vue in the last century. The cottages in the foreground were demolished in the early 1900s and shops have been built in their place. Many originally operated little shops from their front rooms. These were known as 'tiddly shops' because they sold small quantities of a great variety of goods from groceries to shoelaces or stationery. In the 1930s the terrace of houses to the left was called Hill View.

The frontage of the popular emporium known as Flexbury Supply Stores at Summerleaze Avenue in the early 1900s. The store sold provisions, groceries and household goods.

Lifeboat Day at Bude, 20 August 1908. King William IV presented Bude with its first lifeboat in 1837, mainly at the request of the Revd R. S. Hawker of Morwenstow, who in the previous year had started a fund to purchase a lifeboat for Bude, making the first donation of £1 himself. The fund only grew very slowly and Revd Hawker wrote to the King seeking his assistance. In 1866 the first RNLI lifeboat arrived at Bude. Since trade into the town has declined to such a large extent, the RNLI now provides only an inshore rescue boat. This is manned by volunteers and does sterling service, and Lifeboat Day is still an important date in Bude's calendar of annual events.

The ketch *Ceres* in the Bude Canal in 1933. This photograph was taken by the author, as a very small child, using a 127 Box Brownie camera which cost six shillings and sixpence when new!

Ceres being unloaded in Bude Canal in 1936 just before her sinking.

The sailing ketch *Ceres* was the oldest ship on Lloyd's Register and completed 125 years service at sea. She was built at Salcombe, Devon in 1811 and was involved in carrying stores to the Peninsular War. In 1826 she was taken to Bude where she was bought in 1852 by Henry Petherick, remaining Petherick through four generations. She was fitted with a small auxiliary engine to enhance her sail power in 1912. During World War I she avoided German submarines and throughout the war years continued bringing cargoes into Bude from ports all around Great Britain. She remained a fully rigged sailing ketch to the end of her days. Her end came in 1936, in the saddest possible way, when she sprang a leak whilst rounding Baggy Point in North Devon. Captain Jeffery and his crew were rescued by the Appledore lifeboat but despite the most strenuous efforts *Ceres* could not be saved and she sank, carrying out her duties to the last. In all her sailing days she never lost a member of her crews and there were many tears shed in Bude and elsewhere when news came of her unfortunate end.

A huge crowd of spectators gathered to watch rowing, swimming and other events. Water sports have always been popular in Bude, the canal lending itself to such activities, and events such as this were organised on a frequent basis during the summer months. Nowadays the canal is popular with canoeists and small yachts moor at the wharf. The railway waggons on the wharf were used to transport goods that had been brought in by sea and sailed up the canal. There was a rail connection with Bude station about half a mile away, allowing waggons to be shunted directly from the railhead to the wharf. The building on the left is the lifeboat house

This photograph of Compass Point and the coast north of Bude dates from the 1930s. The Point stands above some of the cruellest rocks around the Cornish coast, and a shipwreck chart of Cornwall shows a huge concentration of wrecks beneath it. Sir Thomas Acland had the Storm Tower built on the Point in the nineteenth century; it is an octagonal building, the sides of which are turned to the cardinal and intermediate points of the compass (the names of which are carved into the stone at the top). It has been described as a 'temple of the winds', and serves as a landmark for shipping. The cliffs beneath the Point form buttresses, with huge slabs of rock standing almost vertical. They are of great interest to geologists, as well as seasoned climbers who enjoy their challenges, although the cliffs are highly dangerous, especially for novices. There was once a flagstaff by the storm tower and a red flag used to be hoisted when ships could not enter the harbour because of the tide. The original tower was demolished in July 1881 because the condition of the cliff below had rendered it unsafe, at which point Sir Thomas Acland erected the present building further from the cliff edge.

Bude Fair photographed on 22 September 1911. The fair is still a highlight of Bude's year, but has changed considerably over the years and is now essentially a funfair. In the past stalls selling almost every imaginable type of novelty crowded together and there was also some horse trading, as well as sideshows featuring oddities of all sorts and boxing bouts when the local youths could pit their skills against each other.

Bude Fair in full swing on the Strand in Edwardian times. Fetes and revels were frequently held on the wharf in the 1930s and drew crowds from miles around. A few years ago the annual fair and funfair – a hugely popular event – was moved from the wharf to the main car park, following complaints from residents about noise and litter.

Crowds gather to watch evacuees from London arrive at Bude station soon after the outbreak of World War II in 1939. The children were marshalled in line to a reception centre, where those residents willing to house them would select or be allocated children to stay with them. Some of the children were housed in Bude town, while others went to outlying farms.

FAIRFIELD Rd
SOUTHFIELD Rd
BROADCLOSE HILL
BRAMBLE HILL

VICTORY PARTY
MAY 25th 1945.

PHOTO
A. SAMPSON

To celebrate victory in World War II people from four residential areas in Bude joined together to provide a party for local children on 25 May 1945. Such events were held throughout the country at the time, with residents in each street clubbing together to provide food and decorations for the celebrations.

For many years St Catherine's boarding school was a popular private school for girls in Bude, taking in pupils from quite a wide area. The school was housed in Downs View in property owned by Misses Flossie and Margaret Weir. Margaret Weir was the school principal and is pictured here outside 32 Downs View.

The staff at St Catherine's boarding school, believed to have been photographed in the 1930s. The only person named is the lady second from right in the back row, who is identified as Miss Lucy Player.

Nos. 32, 33 and 34 Downs View, the three houses which comprised St Catherine's boarding school, photographed in the 1920s. The school was in existence up to the 1960s and offered a good all-round education, making it popular with parents seeking private schooling for their daughters in salubrious surroundings. Former pupils recall happy times spent at the school. The principal, Miss Margaret Weir, was said to be firm but very fair and kindly and was well liked by the pupils.

The view from the back of St Catherine's School, Downs View, in the 1920s, with pupils playing on their netball pitch.

Reg, Muriel, Marjorie and Win Fletcher photographed in 1910 at Crooklets beach with the woman who was in charge of the bathing huts, plus an unnamed friend. Those wishing to bathe from the beach could hire a hut for whatever period they required. These were used for undressing and dressing and personal possessions such as handbags and wrist watches could be left in them as they were supervised. The huts were static and not wheeled into the water like bathing machines. In earlier days, when sea bathing first became popular, Nanny Moore would have been on hand to lead into the sea anyone timid about facing the waves for the first time.

'Tommy's Pit' bathing pool was a natural pool which Sir Thomas Acland had enlarged as a men's swimming pool. It was by the breakwater on the site of the former Banjo Pier and part of the sea caves owned by Sir Thomas. The Banjo Pier was destroyed by a storm in February 1838. Although called a pier, it was in fact a breakwater and was superseded in 1839 by the present breakwater. This was rebuilt on the foundations of the original structure by the Bude Canal engineer George Casebourne, and was designed to present less resistance to the waves than the 'Banjo'. In later years Tommy's Pit was used by mixed bathers.

Below: The new bathing pool at Summerleaze Point was opened on 10 July 1930 by the Hon. Mrs G. A. C. Thynne (pictured here). It is an acre in extent and in its building the natural rock formation was used as much as possible. The water is replaced by every tide, and the pool empties in four hours and refills in half an hour. The suggestion that a swimming pool should be built came from Mr Thynne of Trelana, Poughill, who generously offered £2,500 towards the estimated cost of £4,000. On the opening day the chairman of Bude and Stratton Urban District Council, Mr F. Jeffery, welcomed Mrs Thynne. A huge crowd gathered for the event and after the opening there were sports events provided by the different schools in Bude as well as the Devonshire Amateur Swimming Association.

This picture of boys bathing in Tommy's Pit appeared in the *Post & Weekly News* in 1910. Mixed bathing was later allowed in the 'Pit' which was immensely popular with children.

The swimming pool in use soon after its opening in 1930. The pool has always been a popular attraction for both locals and visitors. Prior to the new pool being opened Crooklets beach was designated the ladies' beach and Summerleaze the gentlemen's beach for swimming.

In the 1930s stalls were erected at Crooklets beach during the holiday season to provide refreshments and beach goods for holidaymakers. This was discontinued at the outbreak of World War II and was never resumed.

One of Petherick's vessels at the mouth of the sea lock in the late nineteenth century.

Bude Canal c.1913. Two ships have come through the sea lock and have berthed alongside. Here a narrow gauge rail track was used by horses to haul small trucks up from the beach. The sand they carried would be unloaded into one of the barges seen moored alongside in the foreground. Originally the track was laid as 4 foot gauge and operated from 1823 to 1923, although in 1924 it was converted to 2 foot gauge and continued to be used until 1942 (the tracks remain in place today). The mineral-rich sand was transported to the hinterland for use as a fertiliser on fields. The original idea behind the canal's construction was that it would provide work for men coming back from the Napoleonic Wars and that the sand would improve the quality of nearby agricultural land. At the time this was poor and offered few nutrients for either grazing or the growing of crops. The sand was transported by barge as far as Hele Bridge. From there the canal was narrower and shallower and it was transferred to smaller tub boats. Between four and six of these would be strung together and pulled by a single horse. The leading boat had a pointed bow and the boatman stood in the bow of the second boat to steer the whole string with the aid of a handspike, which he wielded between the first and second boats to control their passage.

All the warehouses on the banks of the Bude Canal have now been converted to other uses or demolished and flats built on their site. Petherick's warehouse remained until the 1980s. The canal continued from Hele Bridge to Red Post with one long incline plane at Hobbacott. At Red Post it divided, with one branch going to Holsworthy and the other to Launceston. The Holsworthy branch was originally intended to continue as far as Brightley Bridge near Okehampton but was never completed due to a lack of funds. It had been intended that the Launceston branch should link with the River Tamar, but it only got as far as Druxton Wharf because the Duke of Northumberland, who owned most of the land in the area, refused to allow it to cross his land. (Druxton lies in the parish of Werrington, three miles from Launceston.) There were six incline planes, three aqueducts and two inland locks along the 35½ miles of waterway.

The wharf at Hele Bridge when Bude Canal was still operational. An empty tub boat is seen alongside. Larger barges were used on the canal from Bude to Hele Bridge where cargoes were unloaded on to the smaller tub boats to work the canal in the hinterland, where it was considerably narrower. The stone warehouse in the centre of the picture now houses some relics from the canal and other large exhibits from the museum on the wharf at Bude. The other buildings have been demolished. *Picture reproduced by courtesy of the Rural History Centre, University of Reading.*

Bude Canal in the hinterland in 1936. The canal bridges were distinctive and several remain today. Both barges and tub boats were horse-drawn, the latter being strung together four to six at a time, with each 'string' pulled by one horse. The tub boats had heavy iron wheels allowing them to run on the rails of the incline planes and these wheels caused considerable damage to the canal banks. At some sharp bends stone walls with coping were built to prevent inaccurately steered boats from ploughing into the banks.

The towpath along the barge section of the Bude Canal looking towards Rodd's Bridge and Lock from the Hele Bridge direction. Both bridge and lock fell into disrepair and all the remaining ironwork connected with the lock was removed during World War II when iron was being salvaged to assist the war effort. Within the last few years Rodd's Bridge has been replaced by the Bude Canal Society, using a new structure of the same design as the original. The lock has been restored as much as it can be without actually reinstalling the machinery for operating it. The towpath has also been improved and makes a very pleasant walk from Bude to Hele Bridge or vice versa.

The Cornish Gorseth was held at Bude in 1975. Here the mayor is seen at the opening ceremony, with the Grand Bard, Mr Dennis Trevanion, beside him (right). The swordbearer holds the sword of Excalibur which will form part of the ceremony, and the harpist (far right) provides music for local children to dance to. The Cornish Gorseth started in 1928 and was based on the Welsh Gorsedd. It was established to bestow the honour of bardship upon those Cornish men and women who had 'exhibited a manifestation of the Celtic Spirit' and had given outstanding service to Cornwall in the arts, sciences and other areas. In later years a new category was introduced for those people who had passed the advanced proficiency examination in the Cornish language, entitling them to become 'language bards' (thus not all language bards are of Cornish origin). Each bard takes a bardic name and the author's is Scryfer Weryn – Writer of Werrington – the parish in which she lives and which adjoins the parish in which she was born.

The Picture House was opened on 23 July 1936 after Mr M. V. Craven bought the existing cinema, which was built at Burn View by a Mr Robert Booth in 1922. The first cinema showed only silent films and a Mr Moffatt played a piano to accompany the action. Mr Craven's cinema was described as being 'palatial' in style and screenings opened with 'soft lights and sweet music', featuring Ambrose and his Orchestra.

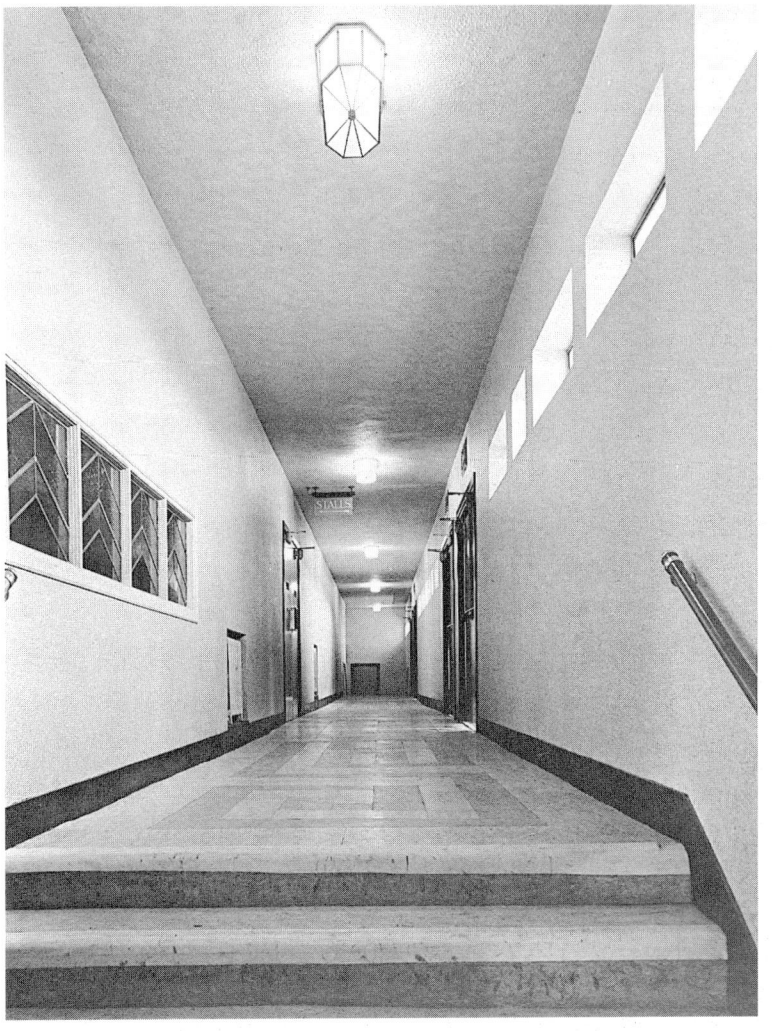

When the Picture House opened it was hailed as one of the finest cinemas in the county. The interior was a vision in the art deco style and patrons marvelled at its design, spaciousness and colour. It was demolished in the 1980s after audience numbers had dropped off very considerably, and a supermarket now occupies the site.

Coronation Day, Bude. 22-6-11. Royal Salute on Shalder Hill, 8 a.m. Broad photo.

On the day of King Edward VII's Coronation, 22 June 1911, a salute of 21 guns was fired from Shalder Battery on Shalder Hill at 8 o'clock in the morning, and just about every house in the town was adorned with flags and highly-coloured decorations. According to the *Post and Weekly News*, 'At 9.15 a.m. the Church of England Sunday School children assembled and it was a most interesting service. The children were all presented with new hymn books and gifts. On that day a grand display of fireworks was given at 10.30 p.m. by Mr Link in the Grenville Hotel grounds.'

Flexbury Park Church, Bude

The foundation stone of Flexbury Park Methodist Chapel was laid on 1 January 1904 and it was opened on 6 April 1905. The chapel is an impressive building in the late Victorian style, and although externally similar today its interior has been considerably refurbished.

↑ ENTRANCE WE USED

THE END ON' PART WAS USED AS A SCHOOL 1941-45 BY { HIGHER ST BUDEAUX FOUNDATION SCHOOL / VICTORIA ROAD SCHOOL, ST BUDEAUX } AFTER THE BLITZ

The arrival of the railway at Holsworthy in 1878 effectively sounded the death knell for the Bude Canal, and its fate was sealed when the railway was extended to Bude and merchants transferred the passage of their goods from water to the faster rail service. The London & South Western Railway's line to Bude opened on 10 August 1898 and was a joyous occasion. The railway's directors arrived from Exeter in a special train and drove in open carriages through a triumphal arch into the town. Bude Band was in attendance to add inspiring music to the occasion and a great day of celebration was enjoyed by everyone. Prior to the arrival of the railway, Bude was well served by coaches. This picture shows John Hamley's Bude–Holsworthy coach loading passengers outside Messrs Brendon's office in the mid-nineteenth century. Tickets were booked at Brendon's office for travel by coach to Holsworthy, from where trains could be caught further afield. The photograph dates from before 1898 when the railway line reached Bude itself.

In 1923 the Southern Railway was formed by the amalgamation of the London & South Western Railway and the South Eastern & Chatham Railway, and it is the Southern Railway which is remembered today as being the rail operator for the area. The famous Atlantic Coast Express was introduced to Bude in 1926. This ran from Waterloo, and its coaches were uncoupled into ~~three~~ two separate parts at Halwill Junction, with one part of the train going to Bude, another to Padstow and ~~a third to north Devon~~. This picture shows the approach to the London & South Western Railway station photographed in the early 1900s. The horse-drawn vehicles waiting to meet passengers and goods off the London train are probably Edwards' landaus. Prior to the arrival of the railway a coach called the *Defiance* travelled between Exeter and the Falcon Hotel three times a week and there were also regular connections by coach with Barnstaple, Holsworthy and other places. Bude ceased to have a rail connection when freight services were withdrawn on 5 September 1964.

Edwards Garage is a long-standing business in Bude and once operated from two locations in the town. Edwards & Sons ran landaus in Edwardian times and in the 1920s Samuel Edwards' Flexbury Garage had a fleet of landaulette touring cars for hire. The company also ran the Morwenna Grey charabancs which operated day trips to Clovelly, Tintagel and Newquay, all popular destinations for a day out. Sam Edwards' garage at Flexbury is still a flourishing business offering all services for the motorist, although the Co-operative supermarket now occupies the former garage premises shown here.

Cann Medland's was a very high-profile business in Bude for many years. It was once owned by Mr R. D. Medland and his sons Kingsley and Gerald. Prior to that the business had belonged to a Mr Cann, who was in partnership with a Mr Greatbatch. The Medlands took on two employees, Messrs Malcolm Ellacott and Vivian Coles, who later became partners in the business. When R. D. Medland died his sons sold the business to a firm called P. Pike, of Exeter, and they left the area. Later Messrs Ellacott and Coles bought the garage back from Pikes and extended it to include a car showroom and an Austin dealership. Some 30-odd years ago the firm also ran an agricultural business in conjunction with the garage, and were agents for Massey Ferguson. That operation was later wound down and a subsidiary called Fuelserv was formed, supplying oil to both the agricultural and domestic markets (the Cann Medland Driving School was also run from the premises). The original garage and house adjoining it were built on the site of an orchard. Messrs Ellacott and Coles sold the business several years ago and the garage buildings and house were demolished to make way for a Spar store. The petrol pumps were resited and petrol is still sold from the site. One of Cann Medland's longest standing employees was Mr Raymond Shaddick, who worked there for 33 years and is now a popular presenter on BBC Radio Cornwall. THE RAILWAY STATION IS BOTTOM RIGHT

Thomas Yeo was Bude's town crier in the early twentieth century. He is pictured in 1912, making an announcement in the Crescent.

Bude's first beach patrolman was Mr George Henry Johnson, shown here on duty in 1912. He also took visitors out on fishing and boat trips in his rowing boat.

A painting of Anthony Payne, the so-called Stratton giant, by Sir Godfrey Kneller. Payne was said to have been seven feet four inches tall and was steward to Sir Bevil Grenville of Stowe in the seventeenth century. During the Civil War Payne accompanied Sir Bevil on the battlefield. He is reputed to have died at the Tree Inn in Stratton when it was a manor house. It is said that because of his size it was impossible to carry the coffin down the staircase, and that instead it was lowered through the bedroom ceiling. Payne served as a halberdier of the gun at Plymouth Garrison and King Charles II commissioned Sir Geoffrey Kneller to paint this portrait.

The Tree Inn, Stratton, where Anthony Payne was said to have lived and died.

The historic old courthouse at Stratton was restored in 1984 by the Cornwall Buildings Preservation Trust. It was erected between 1810 and 1820 as a seat of justice for the former Stratton Hundred (a hundred being an administrative division of a county, supposed to have originally contained one hundred families or free men).

St Andrews Church, Stratton, where Revd R. S. Hawker's father was vicar in the early 1800s. Revd Hawker is the best known of all Cornish clerics, and was famous for his eccentricity and his writings. These included the ballad *The Song of the Western Men*, which is now the Cornish 'national anthem', having been renamed *Trelawny*. It is sung by Cornish men and women whenever they meet together anywhere in the world.